Developing Dictionary

by

Janice Moldenhauer

ISBN No. 0-916456-48-X

Printing No. 15 14 13 12 11 10

GOOD APPLE, INC.
299 Jefferson Road
P.O. Box 480
Parsippany, NJ 07054-0480

Table of Contents

USING THIS BOOK

The dictionary is probably one of the most helpful reference books available. Therefore, it is important that children realize all it has to offer and become adept at using it. A thick dictionary with hundreds of pages and thousands of entries can appear rather formidable to any child. A brief introduction and a few group sessions looking up words will not suffice in making the dictionary a useful resource tool. There must be adequate instruction and ample opportunity for actual practice in the use of dictionary skills. It is only when children can find words quickly and use the information they find with ease, that they will begin to feel comfortable in using the dictionary. Unless students can reach this point of familiarity, it is rather unlikely they will ever use a dictionary except when under the supervision of a teacher.

The exercises on the pages of this book are designed to provide practice in the use of dictionary skills for the child. It is doubtful that any worksheet can sufficiently replace the instructional situation designed for the unique blend of students in a particular class by the proficient teacher. Therefore, the exercises herein are in no way intended to replace proper instruction. They can best be used to supplement and extend the dictionary skills instruction led by the teacher. Perhaps, the teacher might also use the worksheets as ideas for developing additional activity sheets for the class.

Other language activities might be conducted concurrently with the dictionary practice exercises.

1. Discuss possibilities or conduct a contest to name the "dictionary person" used to illustrate many of the pages in this book.

2. Imagine a dictionary could be like a "dictionary person." After students have thought about the possibilities, they could write stories about what a day in the life of a "dictionary person" would be like. The completed stories could be placed on a bulletin board along with a blown up copy of the character. A pattern of the "dictionary person" is provided in this book.

3. Creative stories might be written by the students about the pictures in the seasonal exercises. The students could be encouraged to use the vocabulary words presented on these pages in their stories.

4. The teacher should be sure the students realize that, not only are they getting practice in looking up words on many of the worksheets, but they are also adding to their vocabularies. Discussion of words students have to look up, could be used as entries in "little dictionaries," that each student makes as he/she progresses through the various worksheets.

5. Words from the various worksheets can be used to form spelling lists.

6. Children might also be encouraged to write words they have trouble spelling in their "little dictionaries."

7. Children should be guided in the use of the dictionary as an aid in spelling. The teacher can tell the students a word. Then, a discussion can be held regarding the possible letter combinations at the beginning of the word. The students should write down the possible combinations and then try to locate the word in their dictionaries. This "smart guessing" should help dispel the idea, "How

can I find the word if I don't know how
it is spelled?"

8. Practice in locating words quickly can be
held. The teacher might write on the chalk-
board the word that is to be located, and
allow the students to hunt for the word,
first in pairs, then individually. As the
students improve, the words can be given
orally. Turn this into a game.

9. A message or riddle using pronunciations instead of the words.might be written on the
board each morning. The students can practice saying the pronunciations by "cracking
the code" and figuring out the message during spare time.

10. Children might be encouraged to see how many
homonyms, homographs, or antonyms they can
find. The dictionary can aid in their search.

11. Lists of words of a certain part of speech
can be made (for example, fifty adjectives).
When the lists are complete, the students
might be encouraged to write stories incor-
porating a certain number of the words (fif-
teen of the adjectives) into the stories.

12. Discussions should be held on the meaning
of any word encountered that might be un-
familiar to the students. It should never
be taken for granted that students will dis-
cern the meaning of a word on their own.
All too often, students may miss the entire
point of a lesson because of a word they do
not know and are afraid to ask about. Therefore, it is important that words are examined
in context and children are encouraged to
question those things they do not understand.
The teacher should feel free to look up words
with the children. Students will be much
more likely to use any reference book they
see the teacher using.

THE DICTIONARY PERSON

You may wish to use this pattern of "the dictionary person." Enlarge it using your opaque projector for use on a bulletin board. Duplicate a copy for each student to use as a cover for the dictionary he/she makes. The illustration is simple enough that few students will have trouble drawing it. Have the students make a series of rule posters to hang around the classroom.

First, Middle, and Last

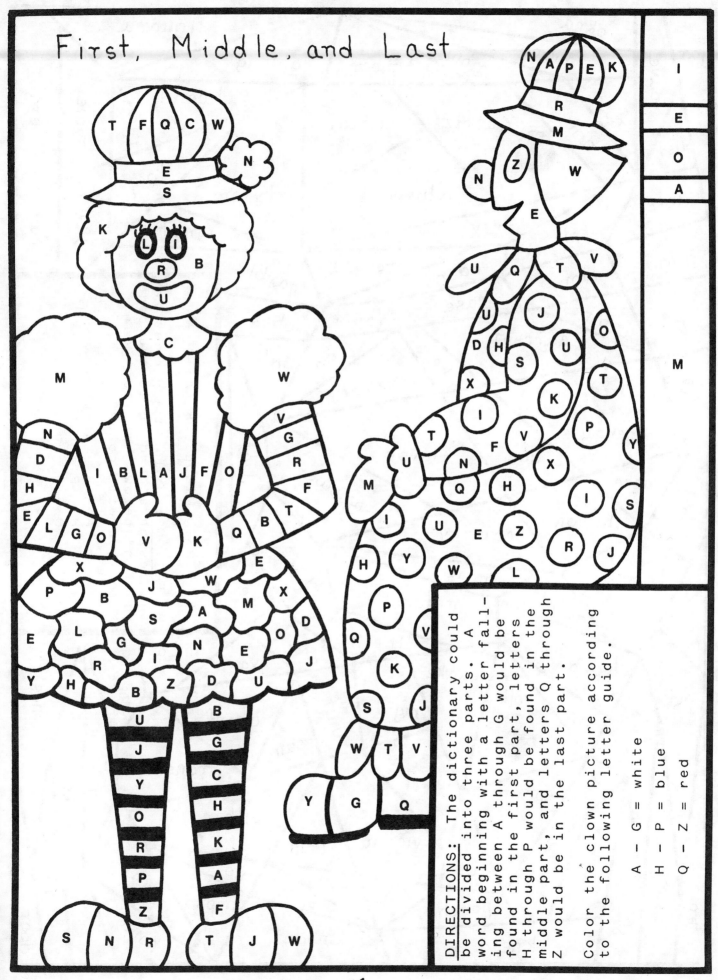

DIRECTIONS: The dictionary could be divided into three parts. A word beginning with a letter falling between A through G would be found in the first part, letters H through P would be found in the middle part, and letters Q through Z would be in the last part.

Color the clown picture according to the following letter guide.

A – G = white

H – P = blue

Q – Z = red

1

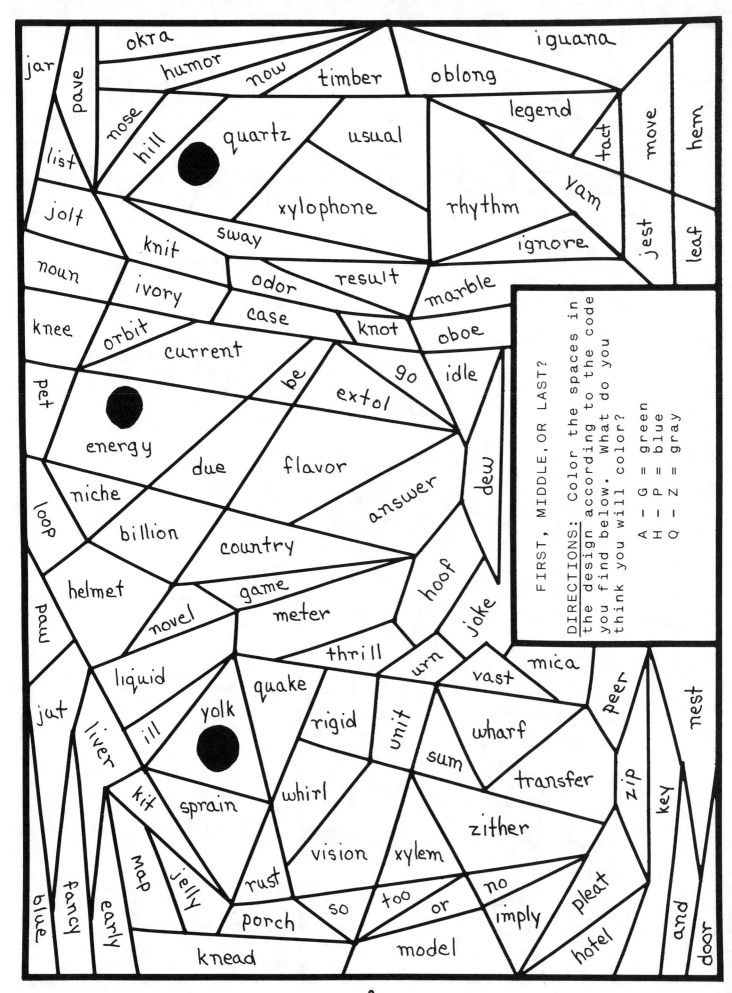

FIRST, MIDDLE, OR LAST?

DIRECTIONS: Color the spaces in the design according to the code you find below. What do you think you will color?

A – G = green
H – P = blue
Q – Z = gray

2

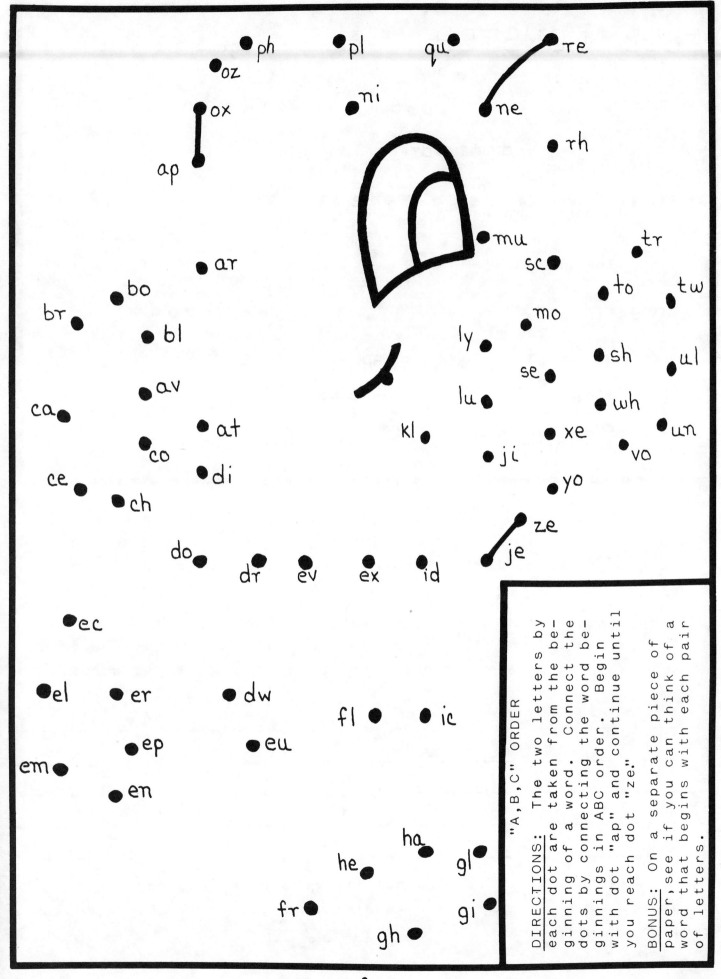

ph · pl · qu · re

oz ·

ni ·

ne ·

ox ·

rh ·

ap ·

ar ·

tr ·

bo ·

mu ·

sc ·

br ·

to · tw

bl ·

mo ·

ca ·

ly · sh · ul

av ·

se ·

at ·

lu · wh

co ·

kl · xe · un

di ·

ji · vo

ce ·

ch ·

yo ·

do ·

ze

dr · ev · ex · id

je ·

ec ·

el · er · dw

fl · ic

ep · eu

em ·

en ·

ha

he · gl

fr ·

gi

gh

"A,B,C" ORDER

DIRECTIONS: The two letters by each dot are taken from the beginning of a word. Connect the dots by connecting the word beginnings in ABC order. Begin with dot "ap" and continue until you reach dot "ze."

BONUS: On a separate piece of paper, see if you can think of a word that begins with each pair of letters.

3

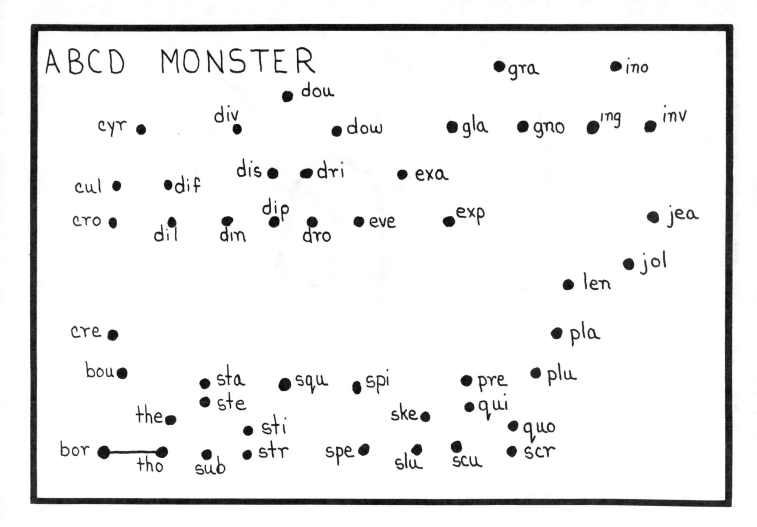

ABCD MONSTER

The three letters by each dot could be used to begin a word. You are to connect the dots in alphabetical order. Begin with "bor" and end with "tho." Decorate your completed monster and give it a face.

You are to write twenty words below. Each word must begin with a different set of letters that are found by one of the dots above. You may use a dictionary for help in finding the words.

1. _____   6. _____   11. _____   16. _____
2. _____   7. _____   12. _____   17. _____
3. _____   8. _____   13. _____   18. _____
4. _____   9. _____   14. _____   19. _____
5. _____   10. _____   15. _____   20. _____

EXTRA ! Write a story about the monster on another sheet of paper. Use as many of the twenty words you wrote above as you can.

4

ALPHABETICAL ORDER

Read the words in the first list. Number them to show how they would appear in alphabetical order. Put a "1" in front of the word which comes first, a "2" in front of the word that would come second, etc. Do the other lists the same way.

___ those	____left	____taste	____at	____sour
___ term	____like	____test	____aim	____sand
___ these	____lean	____team	____ate	____seven
___ then	____lemon	____tell	____air	____said
___ there	____listen	____tame	____any	____seem
___ this	____lend	____tease	____are	____same

Alphabetize the group of words for each number below and write them on the line. If you have alphabetized each group of words correctly, they should make a sentence. Use capital letters and periods where they are needed.

andy   home   today   came   rather   arnold   tardy

1. _____

tame   susan   yaks   saw   wild   two   sam

2. _____

loudly   heard   laugh   harold   has   henry

3. _____

night   cat   mice   carol's   monday   caught   many

4. _____

small   gary   today   seven   gave   snails   gordon

5. _____

prettily   there   often   beautiful   perch   birds

6. _____

ZERO IN QUICKLY — USE GUIDE WORDS

DIRECTIONS: Find each of the following words in your dictionary. Write the guide words for the page that each of the words is on.

1. boast _____

2. experience _____

3. athletics _____

4. golf _____

5. tomato _____

6. quiet _____

7. jingle _____

8. usual _____

Assume that each of the following pairs of words are a pair of guide words. Write a word beginning with the same two letters as the first guide word. The word you write should come before the guide word on the page. Then, write a word beginning with the same two letters as the second guide word. The word that you write should come after the guide word. You may use your dictionary for help.

_____	play --- poem	_____
_____	glib --- grab	_____
_____	lot --- luck	_____
_____	blue --- break	_____
_____	smell -- stale	_____
_____	inside -- it	_____

"HI! I'M ZERO THE MAGNIFICENT!

DRAW an ARROW TO SHOW WHERE I FIT!"

ZEBRA
ZIP
ZONE
ZOOM

DIRECTIONS: Read the pair of guide words by each number. Then read the three words below each pair of guide words. Now,try the following:

Make an "X" on the word that comes before the guide word. Circle the word that comes between the guide words. Underline the word that comes after the guide words.

1. dive - dog
   doll- do - dime

2. jaw - jewel
   jelly - jam - job

3. keep - kick
   kettle - kite - keen

4. radar - rain
   race - rate - rage

5. hair - hammer
   habit - hand - hall

6. star - steep
   stay - stem - stamp

7. dial - diet
   dig - deep - did

8. gate - germ
   gave - game - get

9. fork - forth
   foul - forge - form

10. mine - mint
    minus - mink - mind

11. swing - swoon
    sweep - swirl - symbol

12. twin - two
    type - twirl - twice

13. west - when
    weigh - where - wheat

14. eel - elder
    either - edge - else

15. phone - pick
    picture - phase - photo

16. bright - brush
    bubble - broil - bridge

dance dart	helmet herb	pulp purple	verb very	zebra zinc
base bat	mice might	renew report	wagon walk	quart quick
oboe ocean	grain gossip	issue ivory	noon north	evade exam

Sharpen your use of guide words by playing this game.

1. Two people can play the game. Each person needs a gameboard.

2. Shuffle the words and put them in a pile facing down.

3. Each person takes one word from the pile. The person with the word that is first alphabetically goes first.

4. The first player checks to see if the word fits between a pair of guide words on the gameboard, and if it does, he/she places the word over them face down. If the word does not fit, it should be turned over to form a discard pile.

5. The other player does the same. Play continues until one of the player's board is covered. He/she wins.

6. Should the pile of words run out, shuffle the discarded words and use them again.

TEACHER: Make copies of this page and then make copies of the following page on heavy paper. Laminate. Have the words and the gameboards cut out. Store in an envelope.

dance dart	helmet herb	pulp purple	verb very	zebra zinc
base bat	mice might	renew report	wagon walk	quart quick
oboe ocean	grain gossip	issue ivory	noon north	evade exam

danger	remove	verse	bath	basis
quarrel	reopen	vent	punish	dash
normal	hemlock	nose	excel	waist
queen	island	ewe	zest	grass
migrate	graph	verse	quiet	midnight
itch	o'clock	punish	itch	obtain
hemlock	reprint	midnight	wage	queen
zipper	normal	barn	waist	graph
basis	zest	vest	reopen	pull
obtain	damp	ewe	herd	danger

GUIDE WORD GORDY, SAYS

"Look at the pair of guide words by each of the numbers below. Think of two words that could come between each pair of guide words and write the two words on the lines. You may use your dictionary for help, but only if you really must."

1. college -- company

_____

_____

2. flex -- form

_____

_____

3. law -- lazy

_____

_____

4. knee -- kohlrabi

_____

_____

5. redeem -- reply

_____

_____

6. game -- goat

_____

_____

7. pain -- rude

_____

_____

8. rotten -- rude

_____

_____

9. scat -- simple

_____

_____

10. pick -- pumpkin

_____

_____

11. can -- cold

_____

_____

12. babble -- bacteria

_____

_____

SMARTY CAT

DIRECTIONS: Be a smarty cat and put an "X" in front of each sentence that is not true. Use the dictionary for help, if you need. When a sentence is not true, write in your own words the correct meaning of the under- lined word. Use the backside of this paper.

1.. _____ <u>Okra</u> can be eaten.

2. _____ A <u>metronome</u> might be used by a person practicing the piano.

3. _____ One can drive a <u>jute</u>.

4. _____ <u>Jasper</u> is soft.

5. _____ A <u>pentagon</u> has seven sides.

6. _____ The name of a black metal is <u>geyser</u>.

7. _____ A <u>congested</u> area is crowded.

8. _____ An <u>emu</u> can fly.

9. _____ <u>Andirons</u> are usually found in a fireplace.

10. _____ <u>Stalactites</u> grow on trees.

11. _____ A <u>femus</u> can laugh.

12. _____ A <u>query</u> is a question.

13. _____ <u>Vipers</u> are snakes.

14. _____ A <u>tranquil</u> classroom is quiet.

15. _____ Red elephants would be quite <u>remarkable</u>.

16. _____ The <u>koala</u> is an American animal.

17. _____ An <u>aphid</u> is a piece of farm machinery.

YES OR NO = CORRECTO

DIRECTIONS: "Use the dictionary to help you answer the following questions with either YES or NO. When the answer is NO, explain in your own words the meaning of the underlined word on the backside of this worksheet.

_____ 1. Does a <u>citron</u> tree have fruit?

_____ 2. Can a <u>hydrangea</u> walk?

_____ 3. Is it possible to <u>ignite</u> a sheet of paper?

_____ 4. Does one <u>swelter</u> when it is very hot?

_____ 5. Is <u>chicle</u> used in making gum?

_____ 6. Could a <u>feud</u> be eaten?

_____ 7. Is a kangaroo a <u>marsupial</u>?

_____ 8. Does <u>lunar</u> mean "of the sun?"

_____ 9. Is <u>rapture</u> a sad feeling?

_____ 10. Could a <u>skiff</u> be found on the water?

_____ 11. Is <u>glaucoma</u> an eye disease?

_____ 12. Could <u>kapok</u> be used for stuffing pillows?

_____ 13. Does smoke from a furnace pass through a <u>flute</u>?

DIRECTIONS: Now, try some of your own. Below is a list of words. Use each in a sentence. Some of your sentences should be true and some should be false. Give your completed work to a friend to try.

gnu	gulch	ajar
mastiff	venom	tepid
barnacles	bovine	taciturn
docile	depot	fauna

WHICH MEANING ??

DIRECTIONS: Find in a dictionary the underlined word or its root from each pair of sentences below. Decide which meaning of the word fits each sentence and put the number of the meaning in the blank.

A. _____ Don was a bat in the parade last Halloween.

B. _____ The boys paraded down the hall.

C. _____ Amy designs plans for building bridges.

D. _____ Kari's design won first prize in the contest.

E. _____ Arnie looked at his watch to check the time.

F. _____ Suzy watched the jets take off.

G. _____ Joe spotted the missing pencil.

H. _____ The paint fell and made a spot on the rug.

I. _____ Gina pushed the door open and went inside.

J. _____ People say the twins have a lot of push because they work very hard.

K. _____ Missy helps her father feed the cattle.

L. _____ Jamie gave the birds some feed.

M. _____ We ate fish for lunch.

N. _____ I fished all afternoon but caught nothing.

O. _____ The teacher checked all the papers.

P. _____ He put a check by each wrong answer.

SHE can FISH ALL DAY, BUT SHE WON'T CATCH A FISH.

ZZZZ ZZZZ

WHICH MEANING FITS?

DIRECTIONS: Fill in each blank as follows: Read each sentence carefully. Find the underlined word or its root in the dictionary. Decide which meaning of the word is used in the sentence. Put the number of that meaning in the blank. Sometimes more than one entry might be given. Then, put the number of the entry in the blank first and the number of the meaning second. Use a comma to separate the two numbers.

_____   1.   They put their goat's new <u>kid</u> in the barn.

_____   2.   Fred had <u>scallops</u> for lunch today.

_____   3.   Jenny is to <u>watch</u> her sister while her parents are gone to a meeting.

_____   4.   Tom's pay was <u>docked</u> because he was late.

_____   5.   I will wear the new ring on my <u>right</u> hand.

_____   6.   Angie <u>related</u> how she made the picture.

_____   7.   Ben's bike had to be fixed because the <u>pedal</u> was broken.

_____   8.   Liz said she was sorry she <u>snapped</u> at Mary.

SAME SPELLING- 2 PRONUNCIATIONS

DIRECTIONS: Write the pronunciation and the number of the meaning of the underlined word as it is used in the sentence.

_____   1.   There is a blue <u>bow</u> in Cassie's hair.

_____   2.   The actor will <u>bow</u> to the audience.

_____   3.   He had a good <u>excuse</u> for being late.

_____   4.   The teacher will <u>excuse</u> the class early.

BONUS: What is a homograph?

_____

_____

_____

I HAVE CURLY LOCKS AND TWO LOCKS.

MEANING OR EXAMPLE

DIRECTIONS: Look at the word and read the two sentences below the word. Put an "M" in front of the sentence that tells the meaning of the word. Put an "E" in front of the sentence that is an example of how the word is used.

1. TAMALE

_____ It is a Mexican food made of spicy meat, coated with cornmeal, and baked in a corn husk.

_____ The boy thought the Mexican tamale tasted very good.

2. OSPREY

_____ The osprey flew over the water looking for fish.

_____ A large bird of the hawk family that feeds on fish is called an osprey.

3. GLARE

_____ I saw Bill glare at Ron when Ron took the ball.

_____ It is an angry stare.

4. DELETE

_____ The act of taking out of, or crossing out, is suggested by the word delete.

_____ Joan has moved, so we'll delete her name from the roll.

5. AZURE

_____ It refers to the color of blue, like that of the sky.

_____ Tim wore an azure shirt yesterday.

6. INK

_____ Tammy wrote the letter with blue ink.

_____ It is a colored liquid used for writing.

MEANING — EXAMPLE

DIRECTIONS: Write a word on the line and give its meaning. Then, find a word that begins with the ending letter of the first word and write it on the next line. Write its meaning. Continue doing this on the next four lines. Try to have each word begin with a different letter. You may use your dictionary if you need some help.

Green - a color made from blue & yellow.

NOTE - a short letter, way of communicating.

_____

_____

_____

_____

Now, use each of the six words you used above in a sentence. This will provide an example of the correct usage of each word.

_____

_____

_____

_____

hellopenextogetheragextrapartribegghostubath

RABBIT RUN

DIRECTIONS: Help the rabbit get to the carrots. When you come to a fork in the path, take the path with the two syllable word.

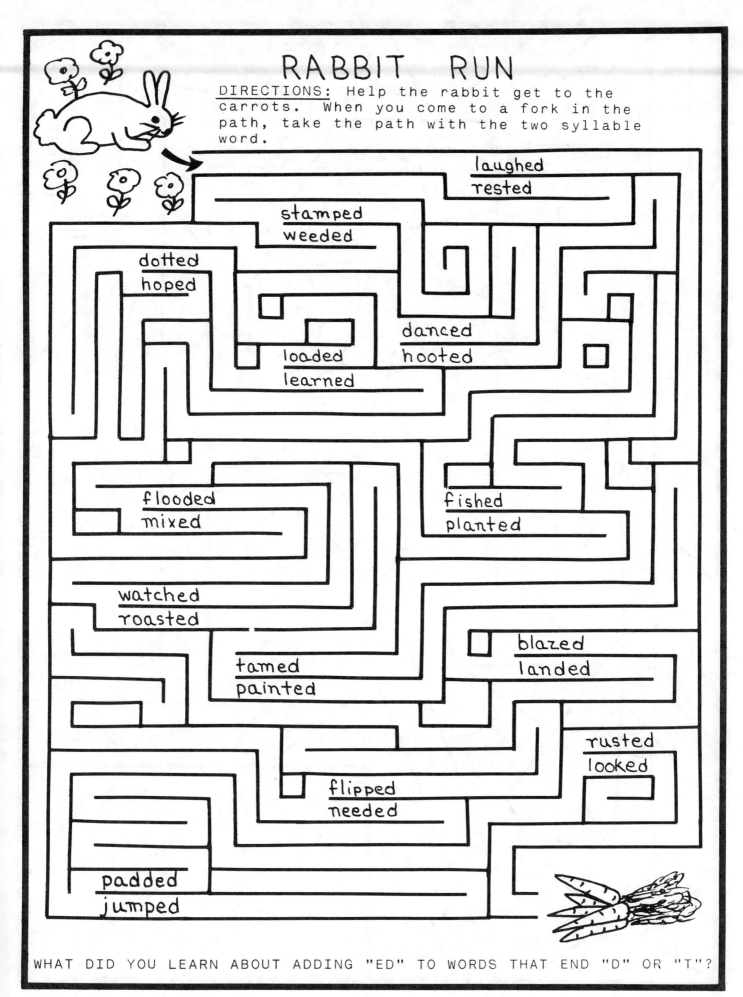

laughed
rested

stamped
weeded

dotted
hoped

danced
hooted

loaded
learned

flooded
mixed

fished
planted

watched
roasted

blazed
landed

tamed
painted

rusted
looked

flipped
needed

padded
jumped

WHAT DID YOU LEARN ABOUT ADDING "ED" TO WORDS THAT END "D" OR "T"?

HOW MANY SYLLABLES?

DIRECTIONS: Color the spaces according to the number of syllables in the word in each space. Use this key.

1 syllable   - blue
2 syllables - white
3 syllables - red

18

HOW MANY SYLLABLES ?

O	V	E	R	M	Y	P	U	R	P	L	E	D	I	C	T	I	O	N	A	R	Y
G	I	V	E	S	A	U	T	H	O	R	I	D	E	A	V	I	T	A	M	I	N
P	R	O	N	U	N	C	I	A	T	I	O	N	S	C	O	M	M	A	N	D	S
P	I	A	N	O	D	E	F	I	N	I	T	I	O	N	S	D	I	V	I	D	E
S	Y	L	L	A	B	I	C	A	T	I	O	N	T	R	I	A	N	G	L	E	S
M	U	S	I	C	A	N	D	W	O	N	D	E	R	F	U	L	P	A	R	T	S
H	O	M	O	N	Y	M	P	O	N	Y	O	F	A	N	Y	S	P	E	E	C	H
L	A	N	G	U	A	G	E	I	T	P	E	R	I	O	D	A	N	S	W	E	R
I	S	S	P	E	C	I	A	L	E	I	T	H	E	R	L	I	B	R	A	R	Y
S	P	E	C	I	F	I	C	D	A	V	E	N	P	O	R	T	G	R	E	A	T
W	H	E	N	D	E	C	I	D	E	I	T	L	O	Y	A	L	H	E	L	P	S
L	A	Z	Y	M	E	C	A	C	T	U	S	S	P	E	L	L	R	E	F	E	R
D	I	F	F	I	C	U	L	T	E	A	S	Y	D	I	F	F	E	R	E	N	T
U	N	U	S	U	A	L	C	O	M	P	L	I	C	A	T	E	W	O	R	D	S

DIRECTIONS: Begin by the arrow and read the first word going across. Decide how many syllables the word has. If the word has either two or three syllables, put it in the correct box below. Then darken out the word in the grid above. If the word has one, four, or five syllables, do not darken it out. Then do the same with the next word going from left to right. When you finish all lines, the words you did not darken should make two sentences that tell you something about your dictionary.

 2 - Syllables

 3 - Syllables

SYL-LAB-I-CA-TION

DIRECTIONS: Imagine you are writing a report and as you come to the end of each line of writing, you meet each of the words listed below. You might choose to put the whole word on the line you are writing, divide the word and put part of it on the next line, or put the entire word on the next line. However, you must remember:

      1.   You cannot divide a one syllable word.

      2.   A word with more than one syllable must be divided correctly between the syllables.

Put an "X" before each word below that cannot be divided. Show where the other words can be divided by writing them with hyphens (-) between syllables. You may use your dictionary to check your work.

1. _____ great		15. _____ family
2. _____ answer		16. _____ Tuesday
3. _____ treat		17. _____ balance
4. _____ straight		18. _____ month
5. _____ picture		19. _____ lumber
6. _____ calendar		20. _____ forest
7. _____ letter		21. _____ table
8. _____ paper		22. _____ truck
9. _____ through		23. _____ sample
10. _____ science		24. _____ school
11. _____ world		25. _____ certain
12. _____ drive		26. _____ terrible
13. _____ addition		27. _____ hospital
14. _____ company		28. _____ tractor

BONUS: Write a paragraph on another piece of paper that explains how your favorite game is played. Leave a one inch (or two centimeter) margin on the right hand side of your paper. Decide carefully what to do with each word that falls at the end of a line. Should you decide to divide a word, be sure to divide it correctly.

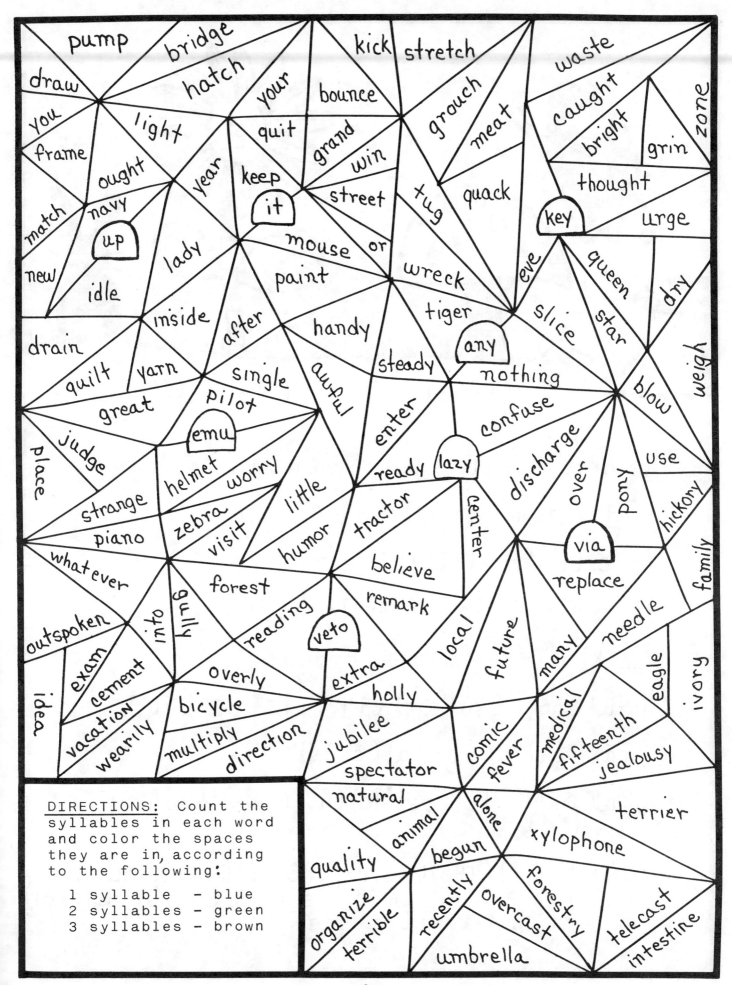

DIRECTIONS: Count the
syllables in each word
and color the spaces
they are in, according
to the following:

1 syllable - blue
2 syllables - green
3 syllables - brown

21

(fol′ō) (THə) (də rek′ shənz)

1. (māk)(THə) (bĭg) (mŭsh′rōōm) (grā).

2. (THə) (bŭt′ ər flī′)(iz)(ôr′ inj) (ănd)(blăk).

3. (THə)(dā′zē) (hăz) (ā) (broun)(sĕn′ tər).

4. (īts) (stĕm) (ănd) (lēvz) (shŭd)(bē) (grēn).

5. (māk) (THə) (mous) (broun).

6. (dü) (nŏt) (kul′ər) (THə) (lā′ dē bŭg′).

7. (māk) (sŭm) (grēn) (grăs).

8. (kul′ər) (THə) (pet′lz) (ŭv) (THə) (flou′ər)
   (yel′ō).

(ĕk′ strə):(rīt) (THə)(wẻrdz) (fôr) (THə) (ə buv′)
   (prə nŭn′ sē ā′ shənz) (ŏn) (ə nŭTH′ ər)
   (shēt) (ŭv) (pā′ pər).

22

SCHOOL   SEARCH

```
P  A  L  I  B  P  R  I  N  C  I  P  A  L  B
G  Y  K  A  Y  O  N  R  I  E  D  R  R  B  O
Y  R  G  L  O  K  E  F  S  L  T  E  A  C  O
W  A  N  D  O  T  A  R  L  B  S  T  S  O  M
I  N  I  O  A  H  U  C  R  A  Y  O  N  K  O
N  O  B  W  C  N  T  P  R  T  G  Y  M  O  O
D  I  R  S  T  U  D  E  N  T  S  U  N  U  R
O  T  P  E  N  C  I  L  A  R  U  L  E  R  S
W  C  G  A  M  E  H  C  R  C  H  A  I  R  S
O  I  R  U  P  S  K  A  A  G  H  T  E  A  A
D  D  N  U  R  E  W  G  L  U  E  E  G  U  L
I  L  I  B  R  A  R  Y  R  K  A  C  R  A  C
```

DIRECTIONS: Below are pronunciations of words that are the
names of objects and people that might be found in a school.
Find each word in the block of letters above and draw a line
around each of the words. The words can be found up, down,
across, and diagonally. List the words you find on another
piece of paper. You may use the pronunciation key in your
dictionary for help.

1. (chôk)

2. (ĭ rā′ sər)

3. (flăg)

4. (tā′ bəl)

5. (tē′ chər)

6. (stood′nt)

7. (pā′ pər)

8. (děsk)

9. (wĭn′ dō)

10. (book)

11. (pĕn′ səl)

12. (krā′ ən)

13. (klăs′ room′)

14. (lī′ brer ē)

15. (roo′ lər)

16. (dôr)

17. (prĭn′ sə pəl)

18. (wô′ tər)

19. (châr)

20. (jĭm)

21. (nûrs)

22. (gloo)

23. (gām)

24. (dĭk′ shə
    nĕr′ ē)

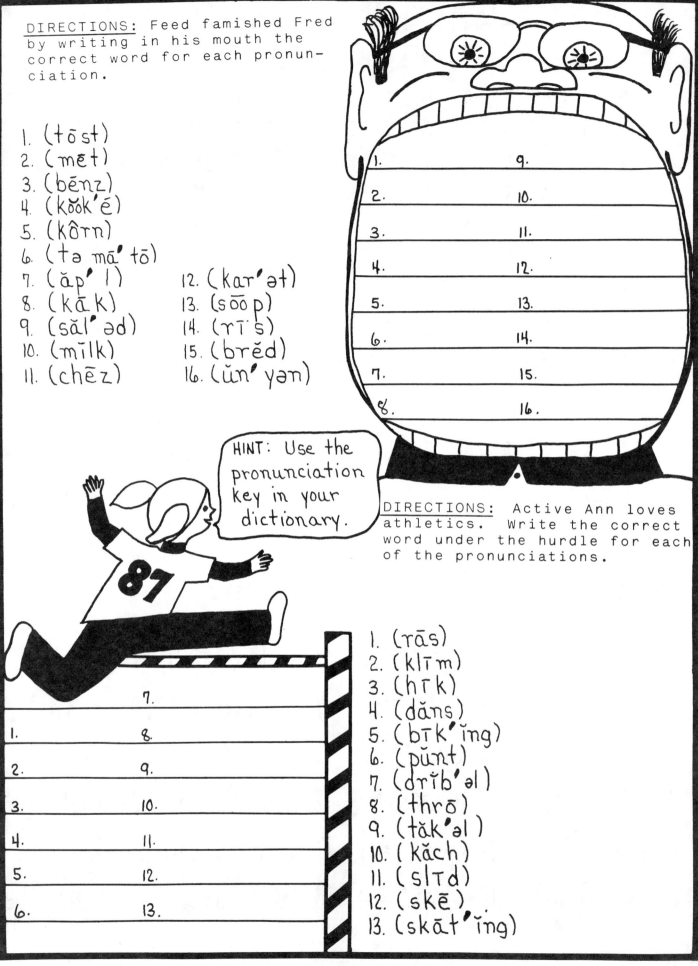

DIRECTIONS: Feed famished Fred by writing in his mouth the correct word for each pronunciation.

1. (tōst)
2. (mēt)
3. (bēnz)
4. (kŏŏk'ē)
5. (kôrn)
6. (tə mā' tō)
7. (ăp' l)
8. (kāk)
9. (săl' əd)
10. (mĭlk)
11. (chēz)
12. (kar' ət)
13. (sōōp)
14. (rī' s)
15. (brĕd)
16. (ŭn' yən)

1.   9.
2.   10.
3.   11.
4.   12.
5.   13.
6.   14.
7.   15.
8.   16.

HINT: Use the pronunciation key in your dictionary.

DIRECTIONS: Active Ann loves athletics. Write the correct word under the hurdle for each of the pronunciations.

87

7.
1.   8.
2.   9.
3.   10.
4.   11.
5.   12.
6.   13.

1. (rās)
2. (klīm)
3. (hīk)
4. (dăns)
5. (bīk' ĭng)
6. (pŭnt)
7. (drĭb' əl)
8. (thrō)
9. (tăk' əl)
10. (kăch)
11. (slīd)
12. (skē)
13. (skāt' ĭng)

24

KITCHEN SEARCH

```
M  S  A  N  D  W  E  C  K  S  K  E  T  T  M
T  E  C  A  K  E  F  O  G  J  U  I  C  E  E
E  O  A  C  R  O  E  G  S  C  O  E  B  C  T
C  R  S  T  O  V  E  A  L  H  G  U  R  A  L
U  K  N  I  F  E  G  K  P  D  C  A  E  K  A
A  L  E  T  T  U  C  E  U  E  G  L  A  S  S
F  A  N  E  S  O  Z  F  C  U  P  S  P  O  L
S  H  C  P  L  A  T  I  S  K  E  T  T  L  E
G  P  O  C  U  L  K  N  I  P  L  A  T  E  S
D  L  I  N  C  R  O  C  K  P  O  T  P  H  O
U  A  E  C  E  T  T  C  U  P  B  O  A  R  D
F  T  K  P  E  P  P  E  R  J  U  K  N  I  F
```

DIRECTIONS: Below are pronunciations of objects that might be found in a kitchen. Find in the block of letters above the words for each pronunciation and draw a line around the word. The words can be found up, down, across, and diagonally. List the words you find on another piece of paper. You may use the pronunciation guide in your dictionary.

1. (stōv)

2. (fôrk)

3. (spo͞on)

4. (nīf)

5. (ĕgz)

6. (krok pŏt)

7. (sho͝og' ər)

8. (kŭps)

9. (klŏk)

10. (kŭb' ərd)

11. (kāk)

12. (sôlt)

13. (plāts)

14. (īs)(kŭb)

15. (jo͞os)

16. (glăs)

17. (păn)

18. (lĕt' əs)

19. (spīs)

20. (pĕp' ər)

21. (kĕt' l)

22. (mēt)

23. (fô' sət)

24. (fŭj)

25

(fŏl'ō) (THə) (də rĕk' shənz)

(māk) (ā) (pĭk' chər) (uz' ĭng) (THĭs) (păr' ə -
grăf) (ăz) (ā) (gīd):

(māk) (yər self')
(kum' ĭng) (out) (ŭv) (ā) (stôr) (ū) (līk). (ū) (hăv)
(ā) (grēn) (săk) (ĭn) (yôr) (rīt) (hand). (yôr)
(klōTH' ĭng) (ĭz) (rĕd) (ănd) (nā' vē) (blōō). (yōō)
(hăv) (blăk) (shōōz). (sŭm' bŏd' ē) (drĕsd)
(ĭn) (ôr' ĭnj) (ănd) (broun) (ĭz) (nîr) (THə) (dôr).
(kŭl'ər) (ĕv' rē thĭng) (ĕls) (ăz) (īt) (shŏŏd) (bē).

HOMONYM HUNT

DIRECTIONS: Circle the pronunciation of the correct pair of homonyms for the blanks in each sentence. Then, write the correct words in the blanks from the word bank below. Your dictionary might be helpful.

1. I have _____ that beautiful _____ before. (sik), (sēn), (sō)

2. He used his ____ hand to _____ the note. (rīt), (rāt), (rôr)

3. Rita _____ all _____ pieces of candy. (āk), (āt), (at)

4. Al put the _____ load of rocks in the _____. (hùl), (houl), (hōl)

5. Sue _____ the bike down the _____. (rōd), (rüd), (rod)

6. We _____ to add the water before we _____ the clay. (nēt), (not), (nēd)

7. I don't dream about an _____ when I'm _____. (ī dé´ə), (ī´dl), (ig´lü)

8. That fishing _____ is a toy, but this one is _____. (reb´l), (rēl), (red)

Connect the dots in ABC order to make the word bank.

eight
seen roar knead
hole write knot
rode at howl scene
ate sick igloo
idol read reel right neat
road need
idea idle rude rod
sew hull ache real
rebel whole rate

27

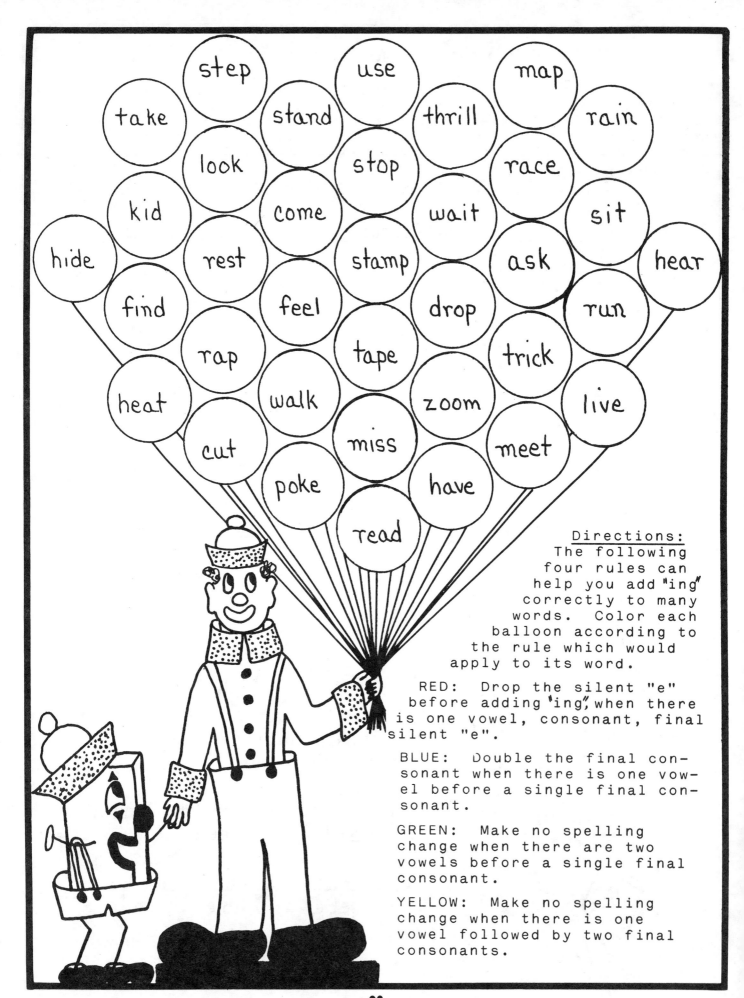

Balloons: step, use, map, take, stand, thrill, rain, look, stop, race, kid, come, wait, sit, hide, rest, stamp, ask, hear, find, feel, drop, run, rap, tape, trick, heat, walk, zoom, live, cut, miss, meet, poke, have, read

Directions:
The following four rules can help you add "ing" correctly to many words. Color each balloon according to the rule which would apply to its word.

RED: Drop the silent "e" before adding "ing", when there is one vowel, consonant, final silent "e".

BLUE: Double the final consonant when there is one vowel before a single final consonant.

GREEN: Make no spelling change when there are two vowels before a single final consonant.

YELLOW: Make no spelling change when there is one vowel followed by two final consonants.

28

FIND THE MISSING L TTER

DIRECTIONS: A group of students wrote the following report. They could not agree on how some of the words should be spelled. Help them by filling in the missing letters. Use your dictionary for some help.

NOAH WEBSTER

Noah Webster was born in 1758 in the col __ ny that later became the state of Connecticut. He was a descend __ nt of the Pilgr __ m Govern __ r, William Bradford.

Webster stud __ ed to be a lawy __ r when he was a young man. However, he practi __ ed law for only a short per __ od. Most of his young adult years were spent as a school teac __ er. He also became an auth __ r during these years. The spelling book he wrote helped stand __ rdi __ e spelling and pronun __ - iation in the United States. Other books he wrote were a reader and a gramm __ r book.

Lexicogra __ __ y interested Webster. He was encoura __ed by sever __ l great statesmen of the early 1800's to write the first American dictionary. Webster worked on his dictionary for twenty years before its publi __ ation in 1828. There were seventy thous __ nd entries in that dictionary.

Webster died in 1843. His rights in the dictionary were sold to publishers George and Charles Merriam. Their descend- __ nts have continued the bus __ ness of publishing dictionaries through the years.

EXTRA: Where can you find more information about Noah Webster and the writing of dictionaries? Write a short report on either another lexicographer or the history of dictionaries.

SPELLING PUZZLE

DIRECTIONS: Fill the missing letter in each word. Then, put the letter you wrote for blank Number 1 in each blank numbered 1 in the puzzle at eh bottom of this page. Do the same for each of the other numbers. When you finish, you should have a rhyme about the dictionary.

porcela __ n   enthu __ iasm   sympathi __ e   furthe __ more
   1   8   15   22

instruct __ r   autum __   papri __ a   mischie __ ous
   2   9   16   23

anton __ m   equino __   stalag __ ite   haug __ ty
   3   10   17   24

pers __ ade   intelli __ ent   gran __ eur   incredi __ le
   4   11   18   25

abs __ nt   tourni __ uet   annual __ y   ob __ ection
   5   12   19   26

finan __ ial   assist __ nt   wheelbarro __
   6   13   20

taran __ ula   seismogra __ h   magni __ icent
   7   14   21

__ __ __   __ __ __ __ __ __ __ __ __ __ __
7 24 5   18 1 6 7 1 2 9 13 22 3

__   __ __ __ __   __   __ __ __ __
1   24 13 23 5   13   25 2 2 16

__ __ __ __ __   __ __ __ __ __ __ __ __ __ __   __ __ __   __ __
7 24 13 7 8   24 5 19 14 21 4 19 13 8   6 13 9   25 5

__ __ __   __ __ __ __ __   __ __ __ __ __ __ __
1 7 8   12 4 1 7 5   13   14 22 1 15 5

__ __ __   __ __ __   __ __   __ __ __ __ __   __ __   __ __ ,
21 2 22   13 19 19   1 7   11 1 23 5 8   7 2   17 5

__ __ __ __   __ __   __ __ __ __ __ __
1 7 19 19   25 5   13   26 5 20 5 19

__ __ __   __ __ __   __ __ __   __ __ __ __ ,
21 2 22   3 2 4   7 2 2   1 8 13 3

__ __ __ __   __ __   __ __ __ __   __ __ __ __ __ __
17 13 16 5   1 7   3 2 4 22   21 22 1 5 9 18

__ __ __ __ __ __ __   __ __ __ __ __ __ __   __ __ __ __ __ !
20 1 7 24 2 4 7   5 10 7 22 5 17 5   18 5 19 13 3

30

PROPER NOUNS

DIRECTIONS: Some dictionaries include names of famous
people, places, and things (proper nouns) among their
entries. A person's date of birth and date of death is
usually given in parentheses.

Given these years, (1848-1906), how old was that person

at his/her death? _____

What do you think this means? (1965   ) _____

_____

To find the name of a person in the dictionary, should you
look under the first letter of the person's last name or
under the first letter of the person's first name?

_____

Find each of these proper nouns in a dictionary and
write a sentence about each based on the information
you find. The sentence should be in your own words.

Marie Curie _____

_____

John Glenn _____

_____

Prince Edward Island _____

_____

Atlanta _____

_____

Yellowstone National Park _____

_____

John Tyler _____

_____

FOLLOW the NOUN PATH

Noun or Verb?

lamp
ran

went
person

played
table

walked
glasses

tiger
rode

apple
did

lake
acted

studied
teacher

send
coat

country
flew

books
built

swam
mountain

pretty
cat

tiny

city

bashful
sun

green

hair

easy
cup

pencil

sharp

awful
duck

beautiful

small

town

turtle

banana
shaky

flower
best

straight
nest

ADJECTIVE OR NOUN
Whenever you come to a fork in the path,
take the path where the adjective leads.

MAKE A DICTIONARY PUZZLE

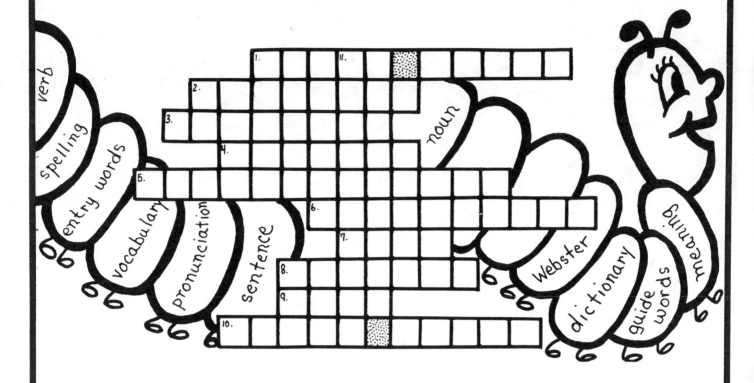

DIRECTIONS: Fill in number 11 down on the above puzzle. Then, decide where the words on the segments of the caterpillar fit in the puzzle, but do not fill them in. Instead, write the clue for each on the correct line below. You may use the dictionary for help, but put the clues in your own words. Have someone else complete the puzzle.

Across

1. _____
2. _____
3. _____
4. _____
5. _____
6. _____
7. _____
8. _____
9. _____
10. _____

Down

11. A book of the words of a language arranged in alphabetical order with meanings.

DICTIONARY VOCABULARY

WORD BANK

lexicographer
linguistics
lexicography
dictionary
etymology
consonant
polyglot
linguist
phonics
phoneme
etymon
morpheme
lexical
vowel

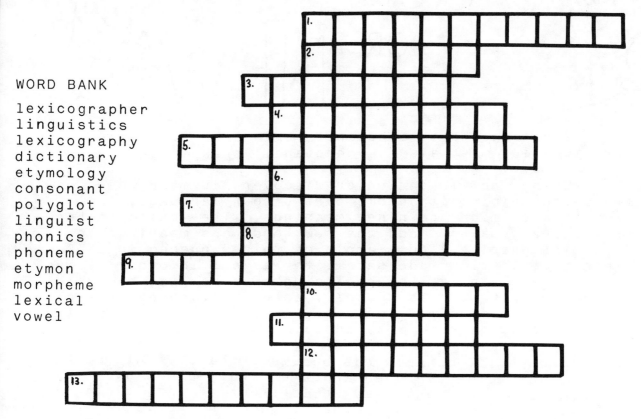

ACROSS:

1. Study of the structure of a certain language.

2. The root from which various words are made.

3. The vocabulary of a language.

4. Person who studies language structure.

5. The act of writing a dictionary.

6. Sound made by air passing through an open mouth.

7. Person who speaks several languages.

8. Word or part of a word that has meaning.

9. Sound made by stopping the air flow in the mouth, then releasing it or forcing it through a narrow passage.

10. A single sound.

11. The study of sounds.

12. The study of the development of a word.

13. Book of the words of a language arranged in alphabetical order.

DOWN:

1. Writer of a dictionary.

ARCHAIC OR NEW

Our language is constantly changing. Therefore, dictionaries must also be constantly changing.

When a new invention or discovery is made, new words describing it become part of our language. "Old words" also might gain new meanings. The lexicographers (dictionary makers) add the new words and meanings to new dictionaries. An example of this happened in 1957 when the first manmade satellite was put in orbit by the Russians. This was the beginning of a new way to explore space. Words such as sputnik, astronaut, moonshot, space walk, and space suit soon became a part of our vocabulary. Many more words were also added.

Meanwhile, other words become archaic. This means they become old-fashioned and are hardly used any more. Eventually these words may be left out of many dictionaries. Words relating to the stagecoach provide an example of archaic words. Early American dictionaries probably included many words relating to stage travel. However, when the train became popular, few people traveled by stagecoach. Then, words such as stage lines, relay stations, and thorough braces were no longer used very much.

DIRECTIONS: Below, are lists of words relating to certain inventions. Put each of the following names above the correct lists: train, airplane, snowmobile, auto, and steamboat.

1. _____ 2. _____ 3. _____ 4. _____ 5. _____

hubcap	track	fuselage	steamer	skis
windshield	ties	aileron	floating palace	sled
bumper	caboose	runway	paddle wheel	safari
transmission	locomotive	barnstorming	smokestack	trails

EXTRA: Make a timeline on another piece of paper showing the invention date for each of the above means of transportation. You may need to use an encyclopedia.

Write in your own words, on another piece of paper, the meaning of each word in the above lists.

THE WORD FOR TODAY

MY NAME IS _____

TODAY IS _____
                  Day of the Week   Month   Date

THE WORD FOR TODAY IS:

_____

IT IS PRONOUNCED _____ .

IT HAS _____ SYLLABLES.

ITS PART OF SPEECH IS _____ .

A COMMON MEANING OF THE WORD IS:

_____ .

AN EXAMPLE OF HOW TO USE THE WORD IN A SENTENCE IS:

_____

_____ .

HERE IS A PICTURE ABOUT MY WORD:

TEACHER: Duplicate one copy of the above for each student. A different student should fill in a form for each day. Allow a few minutes at the beginning of the day for a student to present a word. Then, post the form where all can see it. Encourage use of the word during the day. Save the forms and staple them into a booklet for display after all the students have presented their words.

MYSTERY WORD

MY NAME IS _____

MY MYSTERY WORD IS FOUND BETWEEN THESE GUIDE WORDS

_____ AND _____

ONE VOWEL SOUND MY MYSTERY WORD HAS IS _____

ONE CONSONANT SOUND MY MYSTERY WORD HAS IS _____

MY WORD HAS A (PREFIX, SUFFIX, ENDING, NONE OF THESE)

_____

MY MYSTERY WORD HAS (ONE, MORE THAN ONE MEANING).

HERE IS WHAT I THINK MY MYSTERY WORD MEANS:

_____

_____

WHAT IS MY MYSTERY WORD?

_____

TEACHER: Duplicate and fill out one of the above forms each day. Leave the last blank empty. The students should search for the mystery word in their spare time. The word might be revealed at the end of the day (or all the words for the week on Friday) and then be written in the last blank. The students can fill out the forms after a few days. The forms can be saved and stapled into booklets.

EXPLORING MY DICTIONARY

1. The title of my dictionary is:

_____

2. My dictionary is published by:

_____

3. The year of copyright is _____

4. There are _____ pages of entries.

5. The letter _____ has more entries than any letter.

6. This letter has _____ pages of entries.

7. An average page in my dictionary has about _____ entries.

8. I estimate that my dictionary has about _____ entries.

9. My dictionary has a pronunciation key (tell where and how often it appears).

_____

_____

The pronunciations help me pronounce the entries. The pronunciation key gives examples of how to pronounce the symbols used in the pronunciations. For example, if I see the symbol ü in a pronunciation, I can look at the pronunciation key to see that I should pro-nounce the vowel sound that is found in the word:

_____ The pronunciation (kül) repre-

sents the word _____.

10. Some words in my dictionary such as _____,

_____, and _____

have only one meaning. Other words such as

_____ and _____

have more than three meanings. The word

play has _____ meanings.

39

MORE EXPLORING

1. Guide words at the top of the pages
    help me find the entry words. The
    guide words on a page are chosen to
    be guide words because:

_____

_____

The guide words that help me find "stare" are_____

and _____.

2. The dictionary can help me spell words. Sometimes I
might have to make a "smart guess" when I am not sure where
to look for a word. For example, I can look under the sa,
se, and si entries to decide whether to put the word sacur,
secure, or sikur in the following sentence. Fill in the
correct word.

Dad tied the knot tightly to make the package _____.

3. My dictionary tells if there is a spelling change in a
word when an ending is added. When I look through the information given about the word <u>arrive</u> in my dictionary, I
find that when ing is added to arrive, it should be spelled

_____. I found this information (tell where).

_____

_____

The spelling of the word <u>send</u> does not change when ing is
added. Some dictionaries show how words look with their
endings whether or not there is a spelling change. Others
only show words with endings when there is a spelling
change. Information about the word <u>sending</u> my dictionary:
(tell if the word sending is given and how).

_____

4. Spelling changes sometimes occur when the tense of a
verb is changed to describe an action happening in the past,
present, or future. We say: "I ride my bike, He
rode it yesterday, It will be ridden by Tom next."
My dictionary (tell if your dictionary gives the
spelling changes of the verb, ride.)

_____

BE A LEXICOGRAPHER!

Pretend that someone has
invented something new.
Draw it here.

What is its name _____?

Make up some new words which
could be used to describe the
parts of the invention. Words
that tell what the invention
does, or words that describe the
users of the invention.

List the name of the invention
and the other new words in
alphabetical order on every
other line below. Put the
pronunciations in parentheses
following the words. Tell the
part of speech for each word.
Give the meanings. Have at
least five words.

You may
need to
use some
of your
paper!

DICTIONARY   HUNT

<u>DIRECTIONS:</u> Base all answers on the dictionary you are
using in your classroom.

1.   What is the second word after <u>fang</u>? _____

2.   Look on page 118. What word has the most syllables?
     _____ It has _____ syllables.

3.   The guide words for the word <u>hill</u> are _____
     and _____ .

4.   What is the word just before <u>narrow</u>? _____

5.   On page 203, what word has the most meanings?
     _____ It has _____ meanings.

6.   Is there a picture of a <u>gnu</u> in your dictionary? ____
     A <u>gnu</u> is _____

7.   Write the pronunciation of the word <u>excuse</u> as it is
     used in this sentence: Bill brought an <u>excuse</u> tell-
     ing why he was not in school yesterday. _____
     _____

8.   Could you close a <u>fumigate</u> to keep cattle in a pen?
     _____ Why? Why not? _____

9.   What is the root word of <u>leaflet</u>? _____
     Other words with the same root include: _____
     _____

10. What word on page 147 has the fewest letters? _____

11. Many dictionaries tell us if a word originally came
     from a foreign language. What language did the word
     <u>chauffeur</u> come from? _____ Name some
     other words that come from a foreign language. Be
     sure to name the language. _____
     _____

42

THE FARMYARD

DIRECTIONS: Draw and color the picture suggested by the following paragraph. Use the dictionary for help with understanding the underlined words. Be sure you understand the entire paragraph before beginning the picture.

BONUS: On the backside of your paper, use each of the underlined words in a sentence.

A _feminine_ person is driving a _saffron_ tractor in front of a _chartreuse_ barn. An _indigo_ silo stands behind the barn. A _masculine_ person and an _Airedale_ are chasing a _Guernsey_ behind a _barbed_ wire fence into the barn. A _vulture_ is _overhead_. A _rodent_ _scurries_ to hide from everyone.

THE COLORFUL WORD WIZARD

DIRECTIONS: Follow the 10 directions below. Read each direction carefully. You may use your dictionary for a little assistance if needed.

1. Color the specter pale gold.

2. There is a dappled brown and gray hare.

3. Make the Blue Spruce, green.

4. The pumpkin boy has a scarlet shirt.

5. Color the panda correctly.

6. The crone's clothing is pink.

7. Give the witch magenta hair.

8. The feline is yellow.

9. The boy's brogues are brown.

10. Color the woodland creature gray.

WITCHFUL WORDINGS

<u>DIRECTIONS</u>: Follow each of the 10 directions below, so you will be able to complete the picture correctly. You may use your dictionary for help.

1. Color the apparition light pink.

2. Make the sumac red-orange.

3. The conifer is dark green.

4. The animal that is aloft is dark brown.

5. The witch has a red item she bought at a millinery shop.

6. Her other apparel is purple.

7. The pumpkin in anguish is yellow.

8. Color the caldron black, the pestle blue, and the blaze red.

9. The triumphant pumpkin is orange.

10. The witch has an orange coiffure.

NOVEMBER   SCENARIO

DIRECTIONS: Draw and color the following scene: A
dictionary will help you.

There is a yellow <u>dwelling</u>. An <u>alder</u> with all its

<u>foliage</u> on the ground stands near the dwelling. Several

<u>grackles</u> are resting in the alder before migrating. There

is a <u>cumulus</u> <u>formation</u> in the <u>azure</u> sky. The <u>maternal</u>

and <u>paternal</u> family members look through a <u>confinement</u>,at

the <u>fowl</u> getting fat for Thanksgiving.

GIVE THANKS......for your DICTIONARY

DIRECTIONS: Follow the directions carefully. Use your dictionary to "look up" any words you do not understand.

1. Make the <u>herring</u> silver.

2. Color the <u>maize</u> the proper color.

3. Of course, the <u>husks</u> are green.

4. The male has a blue <u>doublet,</u> his <u>breeches</u> are darker blue and his <u>chapeau</u> is <u>khaki</u>.

5. The <u>scallops</u> are pink.

6. Draw a cloud with <u>scalloped</u> edges.

7. <u>Assume</u> the other <u>crustacean</u> has been <u>boiled</u>. Color it correctly.

8. The <u>tripod</u> and the <u>domicile</u> are brown.

Many additional words, of similar difficulty to those underlined above, could also be used to describe parts of this drawing. Find and define at least five more.

SANTA'S HELPER

<u>DIRECTIONS</u>: Here is your chance. Now that you have completed several pages similar to this page, you can think up the directions. Put on your thinking cap. Find some "super" words. Write the directions and give the paper to one of your classmates to complete.

<u>BONUS</u>: If you want to, you can use a blank sheet of paper and draw your own picture.

A CHRISTMAS SCENE

DIRECTIONS: Draw and color the following scene properly. Use your dictionary for help.

There is an <u>emerald</u> colored house with <u>crimson</u> <u>shutters</u> and a <u>sapphire</u> roof. In one big window you can see <u>brilliant</u> lights on a Christmas tree. A <u>maroon</u> bell is <u>suspended</u> from the top of another window. There is a white mailbox that has your <u>surname</u> in black. A <u>spruce</u> tree <u>adorned</u> with candy canes is near the house. One of Santa's reindeer is <u>grazing</u> on some <u>flora</u> by the tree. Santa, wearing a <u>dappled</u> orange and purple suit, is ready to go down the chimney.

When your picture is complete, turn your paper over and define each of the underlined words.

SNOW SENSE

DIRECTIONS: Follow the 10 directions below. Use your dictionary for help. When you finish the picture, write each of the underlined words with their diacritical markings and proper syllabication.

1. Make the <u>linden</u> brown.

2. Give both snowmen eyes, noses, and mouths of <u>lignite</u>. One snowman should look <u>depressed</u>, the other should look <u>estatic</u>.

3. The snowman by the house has an <u>indigo</u> scarf around his neck.

4. Make the <u>flagstaff</u> silver.

5. The <u>stoop</u> is gray.

6. Draw a <u>feminine</u> hat on the snowman on the left.

7. Color the <u>mandolin</u> red.

8. Make the bird's <u>residence</u> pink.

9. Draw and color a <u>pinafore</u> on the snowman closest to the tree.

10. Three <u>cardinals</u> are perching in the tree.

Carefully follow directions 1 - 10, as stated below. You may use your dictionary for some help if you wish.

1. Color the sign with Peter Rabbit's <u>signature</u> on it pink.

2. Make his <u>residence</u> yellow.

3. Peter is wearing a blue <u>tuxedo</u>.

4. The birch has green <u>foliage</u>.

5. Put your <u>surname</u> on egg "A".

6. Color all <u>wicker</u> brown.

7. Egg "B" is the same color as the skin of an <u>eggplant</u>.

8. Egg "C" has green and yellow <u>horizontal</u> stripes.

9. Make the rest of the eggs <u>diverse</u> colors.

10. The <u>annuals</u> are pink and green.

Use each of the underlined words in the ten direction statements in a sentence to show that you understand the proper meanings of the word. This may be done on the reverse side of this paper.

SCHOLAR'S SEARCH

Follow directions 1 -10 as stated below. You may use
your dictionary for help with any word you do not know.

1. Color all the <u>slickers</u> yellow.

2. Color the <u>instructor's</u> <u>jumper</u>
   <u>scarlet.</u>

3. The <u>precipitation</u> is blue.

4. Circle the <u>mathematical</u> <u>error</u>.

5. Color the frame for the <u>transparent</u>
   opening.

6. Color the clothing of girl <u>ochre</u>.

7. Make the <u>sphere</u> a <u>replica</u> of the
   earth.

8. The <u>galoshes</u> are red.

9. Color each figure of the <u>mobile</u>
   a <u>hue</u> of blue.

10. Color the <u>pigskin</u> brown.

WORTH 1,000 WORDS

Many times words are not quite enough to properly inform
a learner about a word. A picture, map, or diagram is
needed to fully inform the learner. Most dictionaries
contain pictures, maps, and diagrams to help them con-
vey the meaning of words.

DIRECTIONS: Find in your dictionary several words that
are illustrated in one of the following ways in addition
to being defined. Write each word in the correct box.

MAP   A representation, usually on a flat surface, of
             a region of the earth or heavens.

PICTURE   An image, especially a positive print, recorded
             by a camera and reproduced on a photosensitive
             surface.

DIAGRAM   A plan, sketch, drawing, or outline, not neces-
             sarily of exact size,but of exact proportions.

Maps are used to illustrate these words.

Pictures illustrate these words.

Diagrams are used to illustrate these words.

YOU (ô'tō) KNOW

DIRECTIONS: Some words we use so often. We say them or hear them almost every day. They are so common we can pronounce them and know their meanings almost automatically. Other words are less common. Below you will find several words that begin auto. Use your dictionary to help you find their spellings. Before using your dictionary, do as many as possible.

1. auto _____ The story of a person's life written by himself.

2. auto _____ Government by a single person who has complete authority.

3. auto _____ A person's own signature.

4. auto _____ A musical instrument similar to a zither.

5. auto _____ A type of restaurant where customers receive food from a vending machine.

6. auto _____ A self-propelled land vehicle.

7. auto _____ Independent

8. auto _____ The examination of a dead body to determine the cause of death.

9. auto _____ A German superhighway.

10. auto _____ Self-moving, self-regulating

Make a list of as many smaller words as you can think of that can be made with the letters in the word automobile. Do not use your dictionary to help you make the list. When you finish, you may use you dictionary to help you find five more.

_____ _____ _____ _____ _____

_____ _____ _____ _____ _____

_____ _____ _____ _____ _____

abc ABC abc

DIRECTIONS: Use your dictionary to help you alphabetize the following lists of words. Write each group of words in alphabetical order in the blanks.

GROUP 1

awl _____

awe _____

avoid _____

avocado _____

avert _____

avid _____

avow _____

awful _____

awry _____

aviary _____

GROUP 2

seed _____

see _____

sear _____

seat _____

seem _____

seep _____

seal _____

seam _____

sea _____

seen _____

MORE DIRECTIONS: Below are brief definitions of some of the twenty words listed above. Match a word to each of the definitions.

1. a tool _____

2. to perceive _____

3. a fruit _____

4. eager _____

5. an animal _____

6. keep away from _____

7. mass of water _____

8. turn away _____

9. acknowledge _____

10. appear _____

STILL MORE DIRECTIONS: Below are some of the twenty words printed with their diacritical markings. Print the correct word next to each.

_____ sē

_____ sîr

_____ ô

_____ ə vou'

_____ ə void'

_____ sēl

_____ ôl

_____ ə vûrt

_____ sēm

_____ ə rī'

WORD SEARCH

DIRECTIONS: Select one of the following categories:

famous people	vegetables
fruits	foreign countries
human body parts	three letter words

Use your dictionary and find one word to fit the category for each letter of the alphabet. Print each word on the blanks below.

A _____

B _____

C _____

D _____

E _____

F _____

G _____

H _____

I _____

J _____

K _____

L _____

M _____

N _____

O _____

P _____

Q _____

R _____

S _____

T _____

U _____

V _____

W _____

X _____

Y _____

Z _____

THAT'S **ALL** FOLKS

DIRECTIONS: Every word that you are required to discover
in order to fill the blanks on this page begins "ALL."
So, good luck in discovering "ALL" the following words.
A clue has been given to help you. When you finish, see
if you can think of some more "ALL" words.

1. _____ mountains in Eastern United States.

2. _____ what one pledges to the flag

3. _____ supreme being of Moslem religion

4. _____ a rapid tempo, slower than presto

5. _____ city in Pennsylvania

6. _____ a large reptile

7. _____ also called an avocado

8. _____ to let happen or permit

9. _____ to entice with something desirable

10. _____ the day after Halloween

Now, it gets a little harder. The letters "ALL" are con-
tained somewhere in each of the following words. A clue
is given to help you discover each word. Get these correct and "THAT'S ALL!

1. ___ all ___ ___ three beat gait of a horse

2. __ all __ __ __ __ __ __ __ capital of Florida

3. __ all __ __ __ spherical, flexible bag to be filled with air or gas

4. __ __ __ __ __ __ all __ __ great to put in cocoa

5. __ __ all not very large

6. __ all __ __ __ __ __ autumn holiday especially for children

7. __ __ __ __ __ __ all a cascade

8. __ all __ __ large city in the southwestern part of the United States

9. __ all __ __ a dance form showing much grace.